NATIONAL MARITIME
MUSEUM CORNWALL

The Architects' Story

by MJ Long

First published in 2003 by
Long & Kentish architects
27 Horsell Road London N5 1XL

ISBN 0 9543895 0 6

Designed and produced by
KT Design, Falmouth, Cornwall TR11 4RF.
Printed and bound in the UK by
Troutbeck Press, Antron Hill, Mabe, Cornwall.

Copy by MJ Long.
Edited by Sal Wilson and Jenny Bennett.
Photography supplied by Tom Bent, Bob Berry, Andy Campbell, Peter Durrant/arcblue, MJ Long, Krista Taylor and Harry Wilson.
Sketches by MJ Long, computer drawings by Long & Kentish.

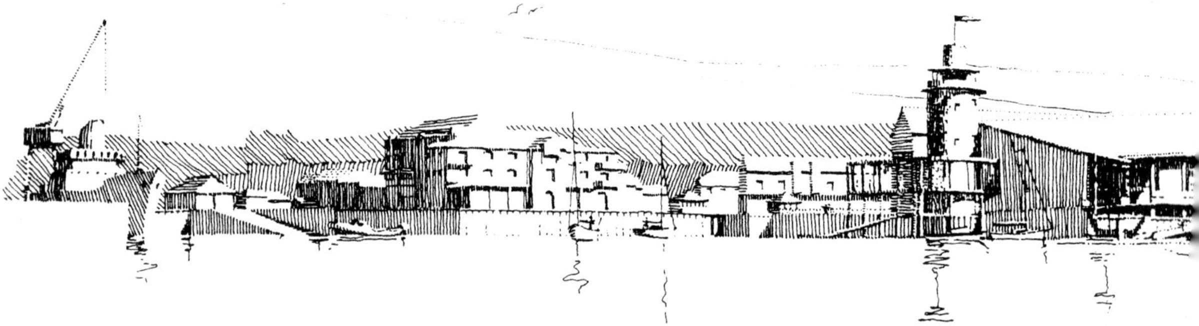

Design is a process of discovery.

Design Team

Architects: Long & Kentish

Engineers: Ove Arup & Partners

Exhibition Designers: Land Design Studio

Quantity Surveyors: Davis Langdon & Everest

Project Managers: Arup Project Management

Contractors

Alfred McAlpine, Interserve, Scena

The building was supported by funding
from Heritage Lottery Fund,
European Regional Development Fund,
South West of England Regional Development Authority,
together with a number of private and
corporate investors.

Andy Campbell

Contents

Introduction

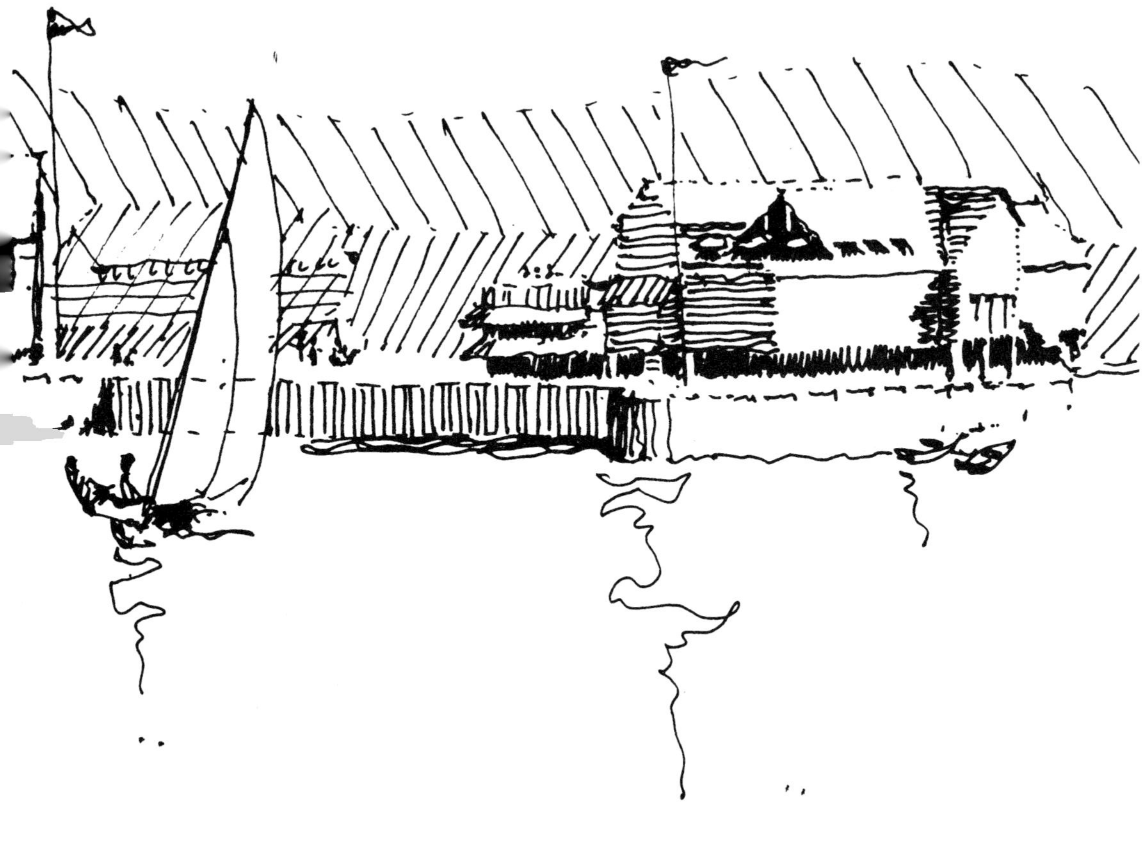

GONE ARE THE DAYS when architects were just given commissions. We all have to compete internationally for any building supported by public money and we have learned not to get too enthusiastic about any potential design job: the odds against getting it are too formidable, at least in the early stages. Nevertheless, when we first saw the Falmouth site in 1996, it was very difficult to stay coolly objective.

What a wonderful site! It's a place where vivid differences meet: water and land, of course, but also the intimacy of the old town docks and the megascale of the commercial docks. It is like a hinge between those two key players in Falmouth's history; it is also at the narrowest neck between the harbour and the bay, where the third waterfront player in the Falmouth story (the beach hotels) is located.

This was an opportunity to knit together and give architectural focus to an important corner of Falmouth and at the same time to participate in a major project of economic regeneration. It has involved work with many local interests and several funders, and it has often been a complicated process. But it has never ceased to be worth the effort, and it is a profound satisfaction to us to see the Museum open, and the 'missing tooth' in the waterfront scene filled at last.

Above: a typical vignette of Falmouth's waterfront today.

Facing page, main picture: An aerial view with the museum site on the far right. Courtesy of Aerofilms.

Cornwall is at a critical point in its history. Its traditional industries have largely given way to tourism and the provision of retirement communities. The resulting economic regeneration that results is crucial to the health of Cornwall, but the kind of building to which it gives rise could easily destroy the very things that bring the tourist and the pensioner to the county. The traditional forms of settlement, which are so beautifully related to the nature of the Cornish landscape, are inevitably being replaced by places designed for people with cars and with leisure.

In my youth I saw such change in New England, where traditional fishing communities have now become Disney caricatures of themselves, and authenticity is largely lost in a welter of sham nostalgia.

I believe that new buildings must indeed be new and must serve new purposes, but I also believe that they must seem to be a next logical step in the continuing life of local traditions. In response to some such comment at our interview, someone protested 'But we want a Landmark building!' Certainly, but that need not mean that the building looks as though it landed from Mars.

Archive photograph of the site. Courtesy of Royal Cornwall Polythechnic Society.

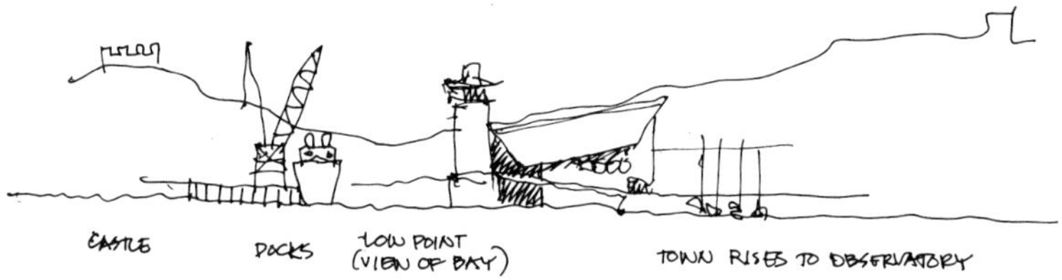

Photograph courtesy of Royal Cornwall Polythechnic Society.

Facing page:
NMMC with the Killigrew monument in foreground.

Context is usually discussed in terms of style and detail. I believe that it is much more a question of the size, scale, and location of buildings. There is no way of correcting mistakes in size and location by dressing the building with style and detail. Equally, the building can be given 'Landmark' status by its placement, without also calling attention to itself by using surprising materials.

What architects do, and how they make decisions seems to remain largely a mystery to 'real' people. I offer this little account of our part in the process of building the Museum in Falmouth.

Below: A study of Falmouth waterfront from Flushing.

Andy Campbell

The order of the following chapters is intended to clarify that idea: Chapter 1 deals with initial decisions about the distribution of buildings on the site and considers their size and bulk in relation to the Falmouth context.

The three subsequent chapters describe the anatomy of the Museum itself, and the decisions about the form of the building that was evolved from the inside out:

Chapter 2 describes the variety of places in the Museum
Chapter 3 looks at the use of natural daylight and ventilation
Chapter 4 addresses the challenge of building in the sea

Chapter 5 considers the resulting form of the Museum building: its 'style', details, and materials, and their relationship to the Falmouth waterfront.

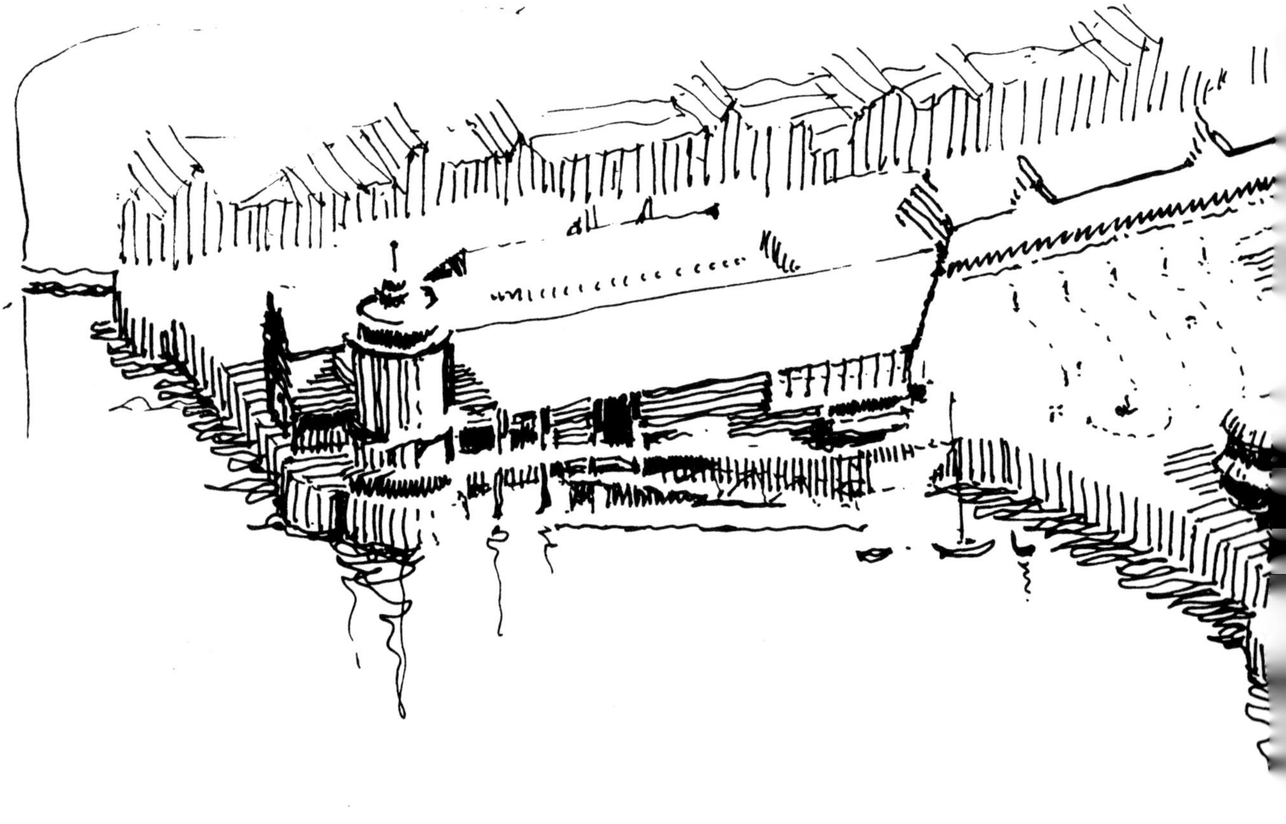

CHAPTER I

The Museum and the Square

ONE OF THE DELIGHTS of this job was that we were not only asked to design a museum, but also to do a preliminary design for adjacent commercial buildings and to use the buildings to define a new square. The square was to be the focus of Falmouth waterfront events (Falmouth Week, Tall Ships Race, etc) and also a venue for concerts and displays. An outdoor room for community events. What a challenge!

First sketch for two museums on the site.

Before we came on the scene, it had been assumed that the Boat Museum would lie adjacent to the launching ramp at the northern end of the site closest to the centre of town. The rest of the site would be an open space, open to the water on one side, defined by commercial buildings on the other, and with the Cornwall Maritime Museum at the far end, closest to Challenger Quay.

We developed an alternative to that, which reversed the location of the two museums, and put the smaller museum closer to town, and the Boat Museum at the far end of the site. We did this for two reasons. The first and most important had to do with the relative size and scale of the buildings. In a series of perspective drawings from the waterfront, we demonstrated a strategy of putting the small and intimately scaled elements of the project closest to Grove Place and Arwenack Manor, and the largest as a transition to the commercial docks. There was also the commercial necessity to draw the large numbers of people going to the Boat Museum past the doors of the smaller museum and the shops in the square.

The nature of the square itself was the subject of much discussion both with the Museum and the private developers. We felt that there was

more to this square than simply providing uninterrupted views of the harbour. We thought that the site should be as enticing in February as in August and that it should work as well in bad as in good weather. Uniquely in Falmouth, this site gets late afternoon sunlight. Sitting in chilly shade in the popular pubs on Custom House Quay, there is a clear view of the museum still bathed in sun.

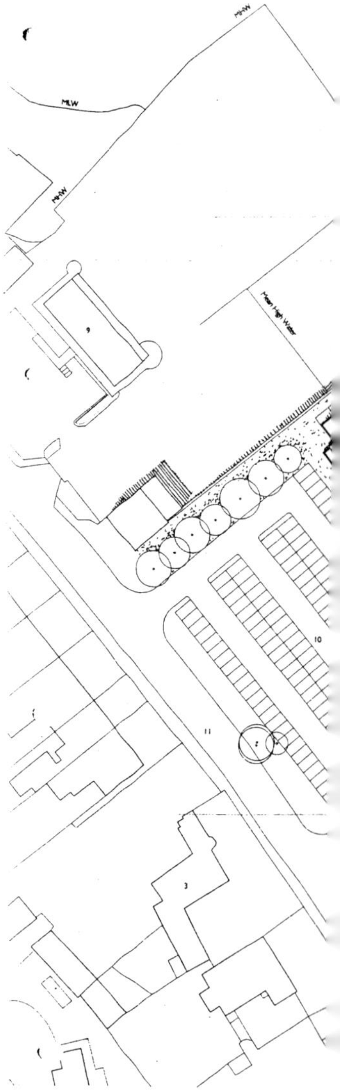

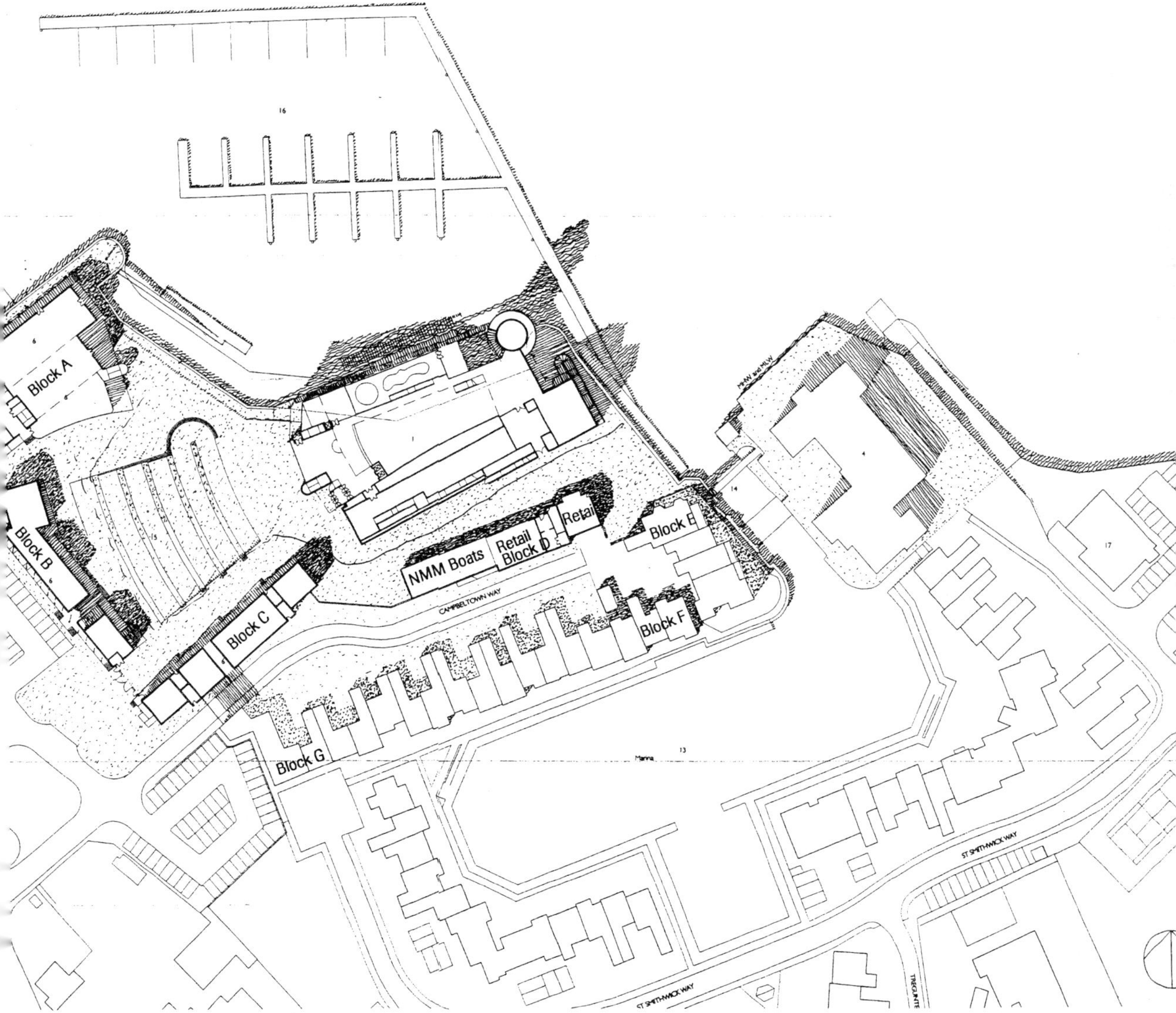
Block A
Block B
Block C
NMM Boats
Retail
Block D
Retail
Block E
Block F
Block G
CAMPBELTOWN WAY
ST SMITHWICK WAY
ST SMITHWICK WAY
Marina

We used sun path analysis of the site at different times of day and year to be sure that in addition to the open breezy views of the harbour (such a pleasure in July and August), we also had south facing walls out of the prevailing wind that would be entirely comfortable for an outdoor snack in February and March.

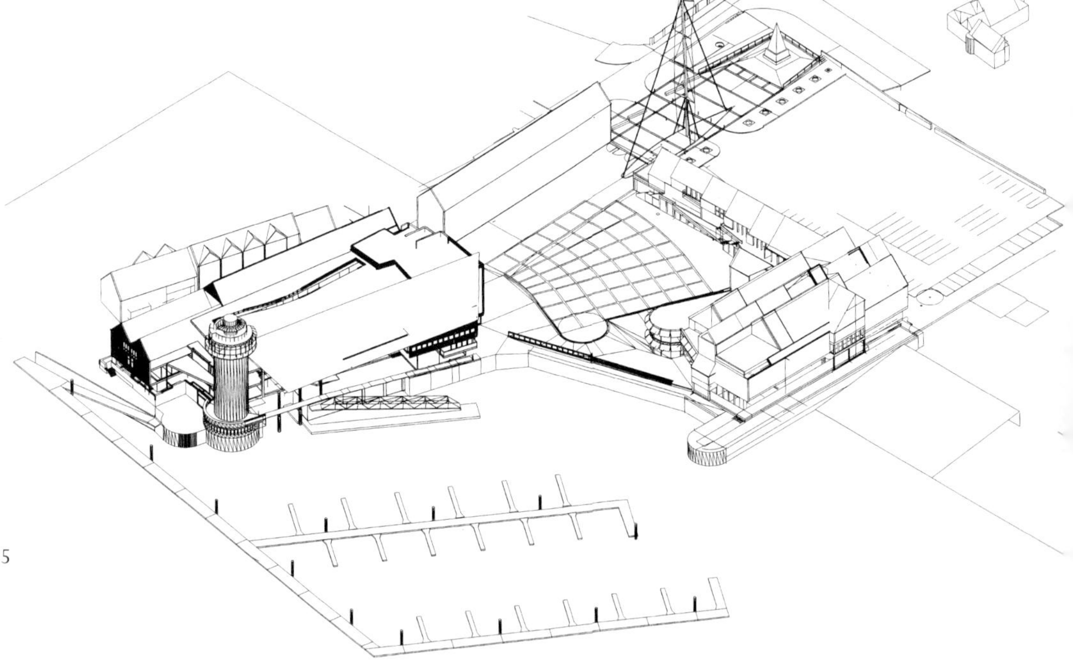

The museum forms the 'stage house' for performances in the square, and its curved entrance facade is designed with that in mind.

Peter Durrant/arcblue

Above:
First sketch of the square.

This general site strategy was retained through several changes in the contents of the buildings. Three different applications were made to the Heritage Lottery Fund, in the course of which they made several recommendations, including combining the two museums into a single building. The finally agreed form was represented in a bass wood model

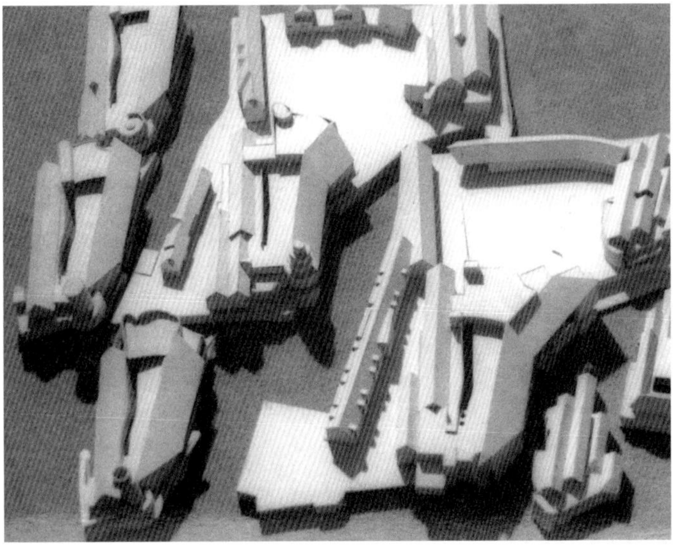

Development models.

demonstrating the intended character of the place. We have been responsible for carrying the museum building through to completion, and have done the basic design for the commercial buildings that will be constructed by private developers.

Below: Commercial buildings as a container for the square.

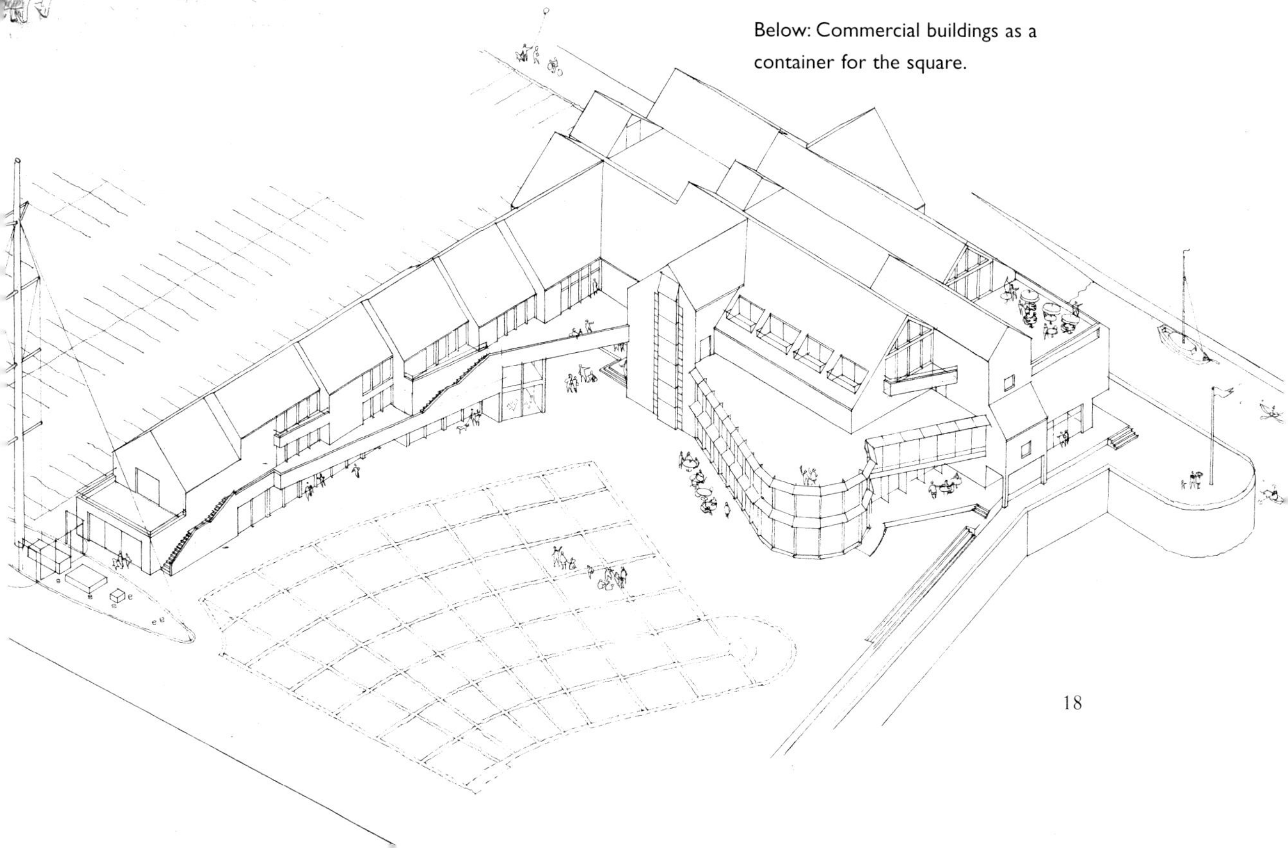

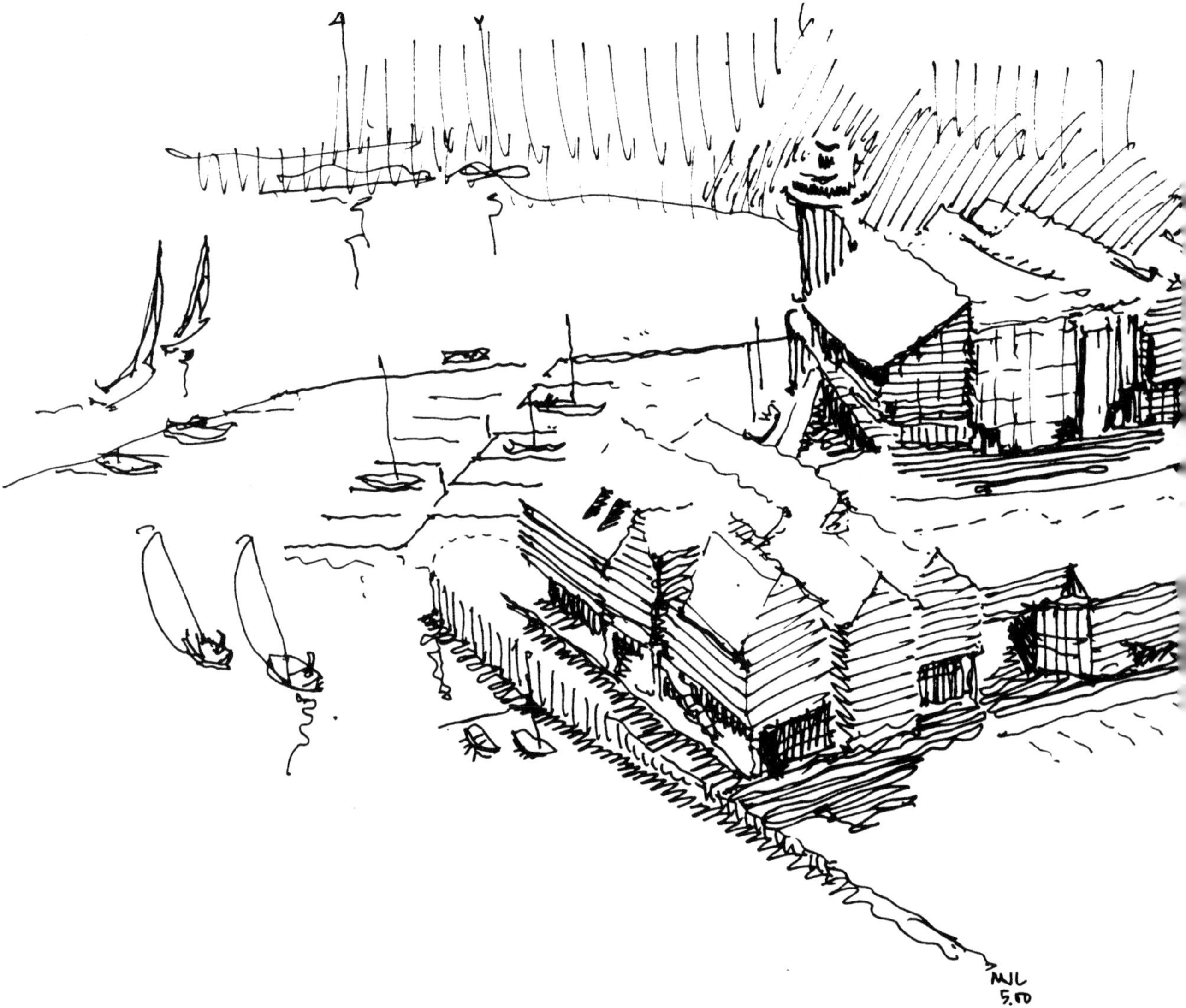
MJL
5.00

CHAPTER 2

The Museum: From Inside Out

THE PREVIOUS CHAPTER DESCRIBED the reasons for the location of the museum on the site, but its particular shape and configuration are essentially tied up with how it works and what happens inside. The shapes are not surface styling (although they produce a picturesque result); but come out of an interior anatomy intended to be both clear and vivid to the visitor.

The museum building is itself an essential part of the visitor's experience. It is not just there as an abstract container for the boats and the local history collection; it participates in both. It is on the waterfront, and it is an active part of the harbour.

It seemed important to us that the building should be as much about wind and tide as about the museum's artefacts. Boats are not best

1. Entrance & ticketing
2. Shop
3. Cornwall Galleries
4. Set Sail
   (Dark Gallery and core boats)
5. Flotilla (daylit)
6. Model boats
7. Pontoon (boats in the water)
8. Tidal pool
9. Tower with Tidal Gallery
   at base
10. Construction
   (2 other galleries over)
11. Library (School Room over)

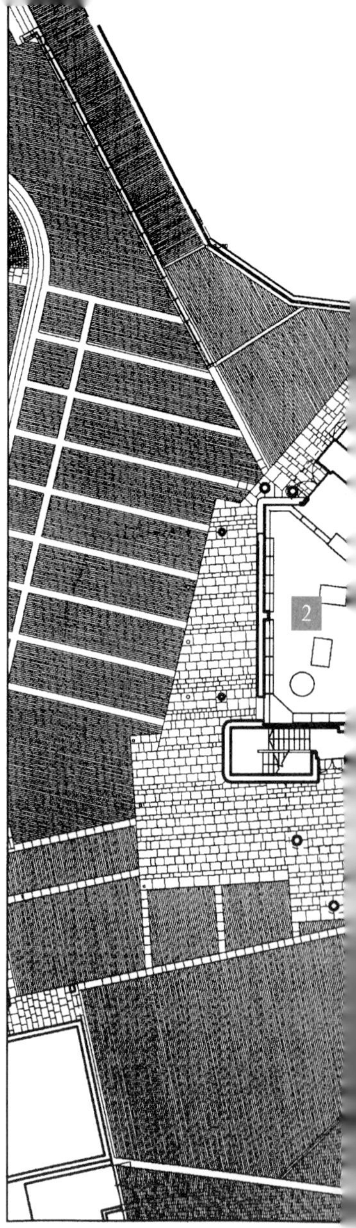

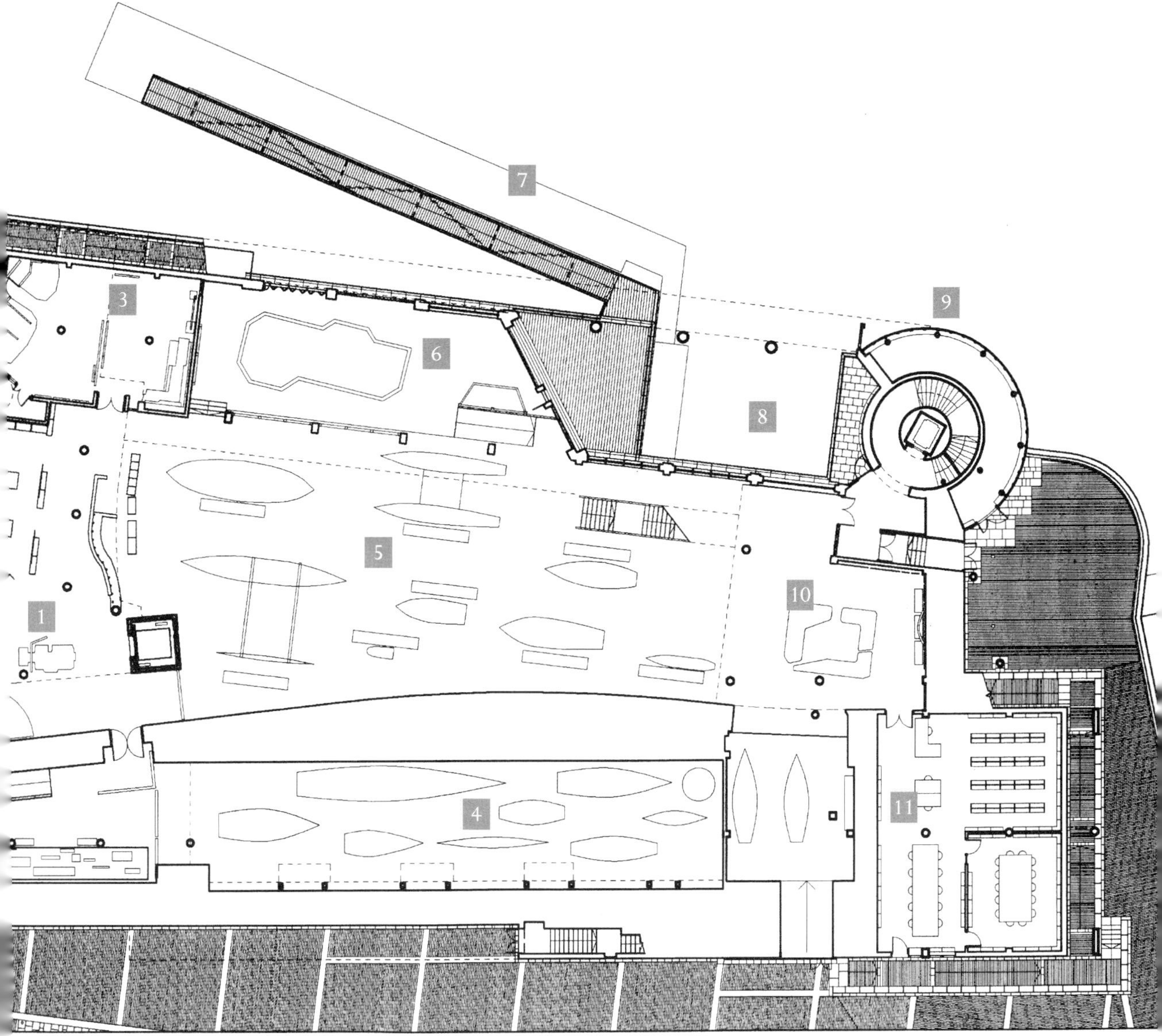

7
3
6
9
8
5
10
1
4
11

Peter Durrant/arcblue

The dark gallery and the daylit gallery.

Bob Berry

understood as static objects in a museum: their shape and construction are directly related to their dynamic life in the water. An understanding of the constantly changing forces of nature in the harbour is essential for comprehending both boat design and the development of Cornwall. This is not a museum which could be anywhere else. It is essentially connected to its location and in that sense is an authentic part of it.

The exhibition designers, Land Design, welcomed that interpretation of the museum, and agreed to work with it. The collaboration with them enabled us to design a building which had positive architectural character throughout. The building has in fact become a 'player' in the exhibition story. We developed the building as a series of very different environments, each a unique place related to the exhibition contents.

The architectural experience unfolds as the visitor moves through the building along the ramps that link all the gallery levels.

The introduction to the exhibitions is highly theatrical. The front- and back-projected images of the audio visual display in 'Set Sail' function as a backdrop to a small number of key boats that represent the different threads in the boat collection. This is a 'black box' in the true sense.

Bob Berry

The boat galleries then draw the visitor towards the harbour. In the centre of the building is a grand hall, with a fleet of 60 boats sailing from end to end, most of them suspended from a ceiling 12 metres above.

This grand hall is bracketed at either end by smaller galleries, boat workshop, library, education room, restaurant, and lecture theatre.

Along the waterfront facade, the building entices the visitor into direct contact with the harbour. This gallery contains a huge model boat pool adjacent to an outdoor deck and a pontoon, with some of the museum's boats in the water.

The local history galleries have their own harbourside balcony opening from the more intimate galleries that suit their collections.

The vital connection to the harbour is most vivid where the building extends its roof over the water. The drama of wind and water are captured in the tower. At the top of the tower is a gallery from which both the harbour and the bay are visible.

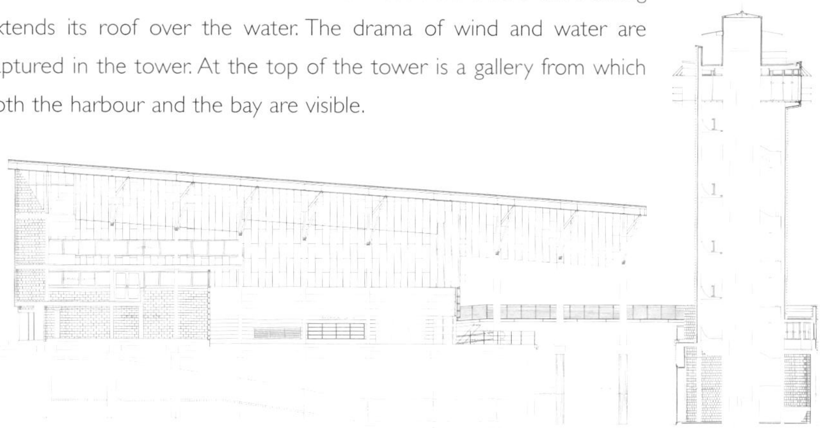

Above:
The view towards Falmouth and Flushing from the tower.

Above left:
The model boat pool.

Left:
The main gallery.

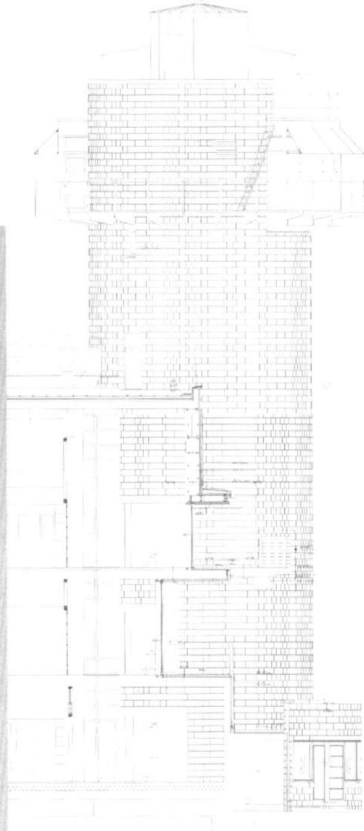

From the town, Carrick Roads, St. Mawes, Falmouth, and Flushing can all be compared with maps of their historic development. There will be a weather station at the top of the tower, relaying current weather information to the meteorology interactives directly below.

Bob Berry

Bob Berry

At the bottom of the tower is the Tidal Zone gallery whose windows are the height of a High Spring Tide (5 metres), so they are completely under water at most high tides, giving an entrancing view of fish, the underside of boats, and even the odd diving cormorant. The windows are narrowed to cope with the increase in water pressure at depth.

Facing page:
The museum pontoon.

Tom Bent

Peter Durrant/arcblue

Land Design Studio

The Restaurant overlooks the model boat pool and on the same floor is the lecture theatre.

The galleries of the Cornwall Museum are smaller in scale as befits their local history collections, where stories of Cornish ships and men are told in intimate surroundings.

Peter Durrant/arcblue

The schoolroom with its adjacent outside balcony overlook the open water reserved for tugs bound for County Wharf. This open water is an essential feature for the Museum where they can schedule boat demonstrations.

A library provides a valuable resource for the maritime scholar.

The shop is located by the entrance and by the ticket desk. The furniture in this area was designed simply in birch plywood.

Peter Durrant/arcblue

This is a building that tells a specific story with a collection rich in physical objects (including the boats themselves). We didn't have to speculate or create effects. We were able to make the museum out of special places: large/small, light/dark, open/closed, wet/dry with confidence: we knew how each place would work with each part of the exhibition.

Bob Berry

Instead of making the building a neutral container, we could make an architecture of different places, of contrast, in which the architectural experience is constantly refreshed. This building is, in fact, an essential part of the exhibition message. It also participates in Falmouth by giving glimpses of the harbour from new and unexpected vantage points, providing a fresh understanding of the existing waterfront.

CHAPTER 3

Designing with Daylight: Low Energy

DAYLIGHT IS AN IMPORTANT PRESENCE in the building. Except in the galleries designed for paintings and works on paper, this is not a museum of even, low contrast lighting.

The use of daylight is a part of the unfolding experience from entrance to waterfront. The audio visual introduction, of course, requires a totally

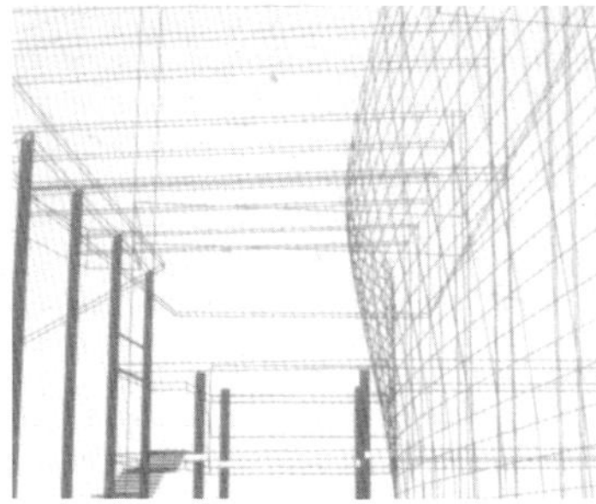

Developing the geometry of the curved wall

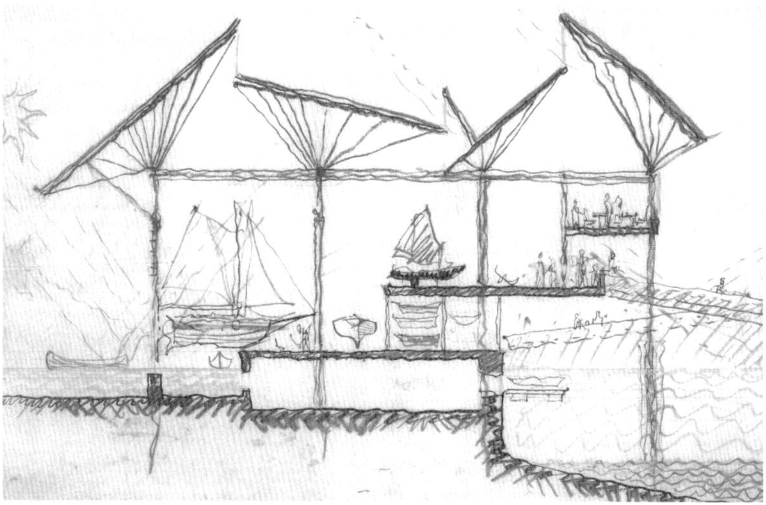

The first sketch.

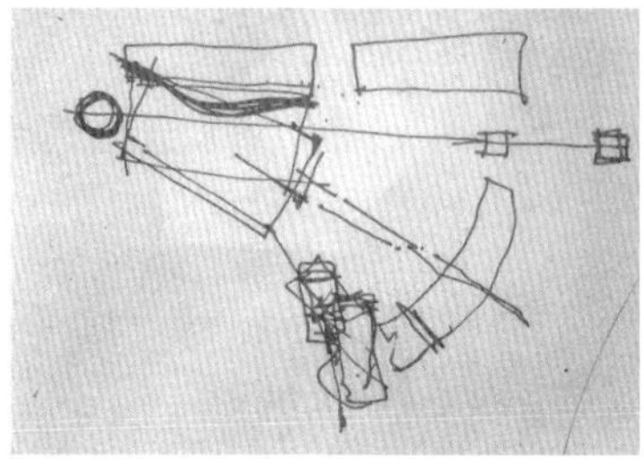

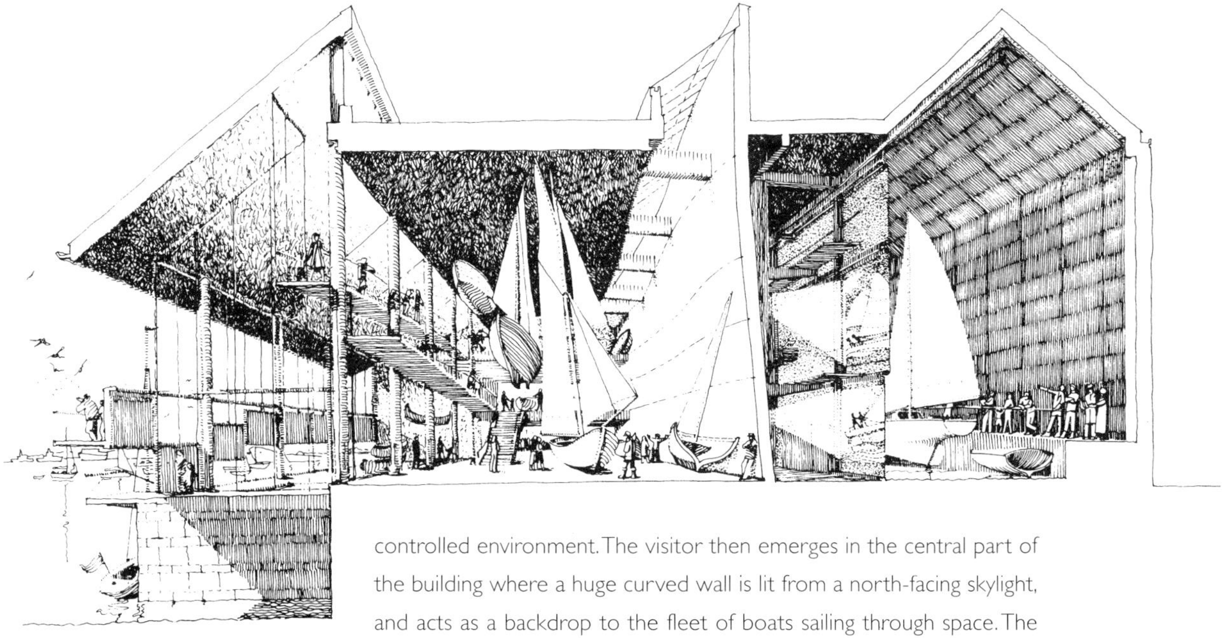

(South is to the right)

controlled environment. The visitor then emerges in the central part of the building where a huge curved wall is lit from a north-facing skylight, and acts as a backdrop to the fleet of boats sailing through space. The curve is intended to emphasize the special nature of the wall. It is at the heart of the building, and helps to adjust and resolve the dual axes of the museum and the square. The use of computers makes it much easier to design and build such forms than it would have been only a few years ago.

The waterfront gallery is lit from above by south-facing clerestory windows. The building faces north across the harbour, and normally, therefore, will not benefit from the reflections of sun off water. To make up for that, trays of water are placed on the roof below the clerestory

Below:
The air flow through the museum mid season and summer examples.
Courtesy of Ove Arup & Partners.

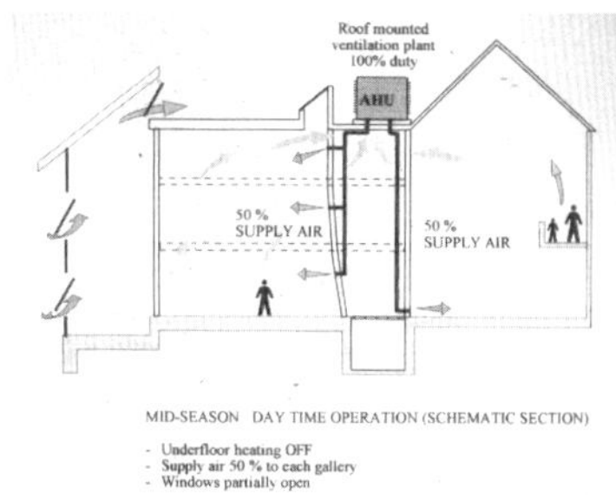

windows, so that the moving dappled sunlight hits the sloping ceiling over the gallery below. The building's developing narrative from theatrical to real is reinforced by the developing daylight design from artificial to natural.

Aside from the undeniable value of daylight and sunlight for the human spirit, its use is an essential part of any responsible low-energy building design.

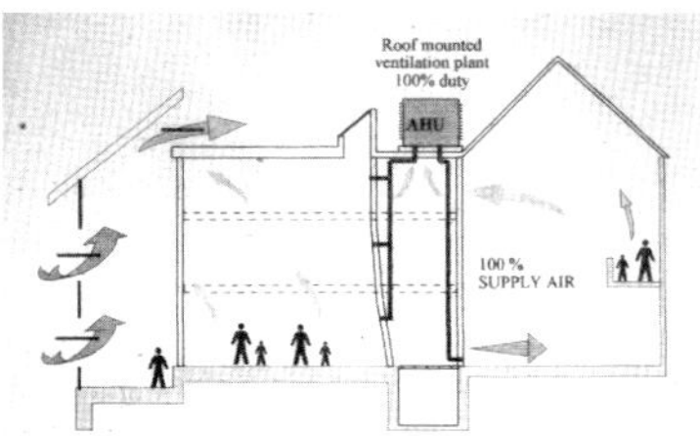

SUMMER DAY TIME OPERATION (SCHEMATIC SECTION)

- Underfloor heating OFF
- Supply air 100 % to the dark gallery
- Windows fully open

Typically, because of the level of environmental control required, museum buildings are sealed and fully air conditioned. In contrast, this museum will be a low-energy building to run. It is largely naturally ventilated, with big doors and louvres on the waterfront, and the curved wall acts as an air plenum. Good insulation and care in the location of openings are designed to keep heat gain under control. Heating is underfloor to keep the walls clear for exhibition displays.

The Temporary Exhibition Gallery and the Packet Gallery are the exceptions. They are fully air-conditioned to the standards required for loans of works on paper. For acoustic reasons, the large audio visual gallery has had to be sealed and mechanically ventilated.

CHAPTER 4

Building in the Water

WE WERE ASKED TO DESIGN a building to last 100 years. A tall order on the seafront! The choice of materials is largely natural: English green oak, granite and slate, because these have inherently good life-expectancy with very little maintenance. All the exterior metal fixings are stainless steel.

Part of the building is built out into the harbour and this called for some specialist engineering from Arup. The original sea wall on the site was

Peter Durrant/arcblue

designed in such a way that, below half tide, a nasty concrete shelf was exposed. Since we wanted water to come right up to the building, we decided to swing it outboard of the existing sea wall, so that it would have its feet in the water at all states of the tide.

Harry Wilson

Hard Hat Photography

Hard Hat Photography

The construction of the tidal gallery was particularly interesting, since we had first to build a watertight steel coffer dam to create a dry construction site until the gallery was completed.

Crown Copyright

CHAPTER 5

Style: Details and Materials

I HAVE BEEN DESCRIBING what the building IS. But what does it look like? How would I describe its style, and why does it look the way it does?

Photograph courtesy of Royal Cornwall Polytechnic Society.

The roots of its style lie in the history of Falmouth. The site was always a sand bar partly covered in tidal pools, and was a natural protected place for shipbuilding on the beach. Later, buildings began to fill the shoreline, and a photograph taken in the 1870s shows a collection of big sheds in which timber merchants and shipbuilders worked for many years. The simple industrial vernacular of these pitch-roofed sheds formed a coherent architectural scene rather different from both the residential and commercial streets of the nearby town.

The form of the museum is partly inspired by these simple, large weatherboarded sheds. After all, in some ways, it is a big boat shed itself, and the scale of a big shed seemed right, placed as it is in closer

conjunction to the commercial docks than to the town centre. But the precedent is not taken over without transformation. The southern block of the museum is most like one of those sheds, and the quotation is most directly seen here, but in fact the language changes as the building takes on a different role on each facade. The shed-like south facade is where boats will go in and out of the museum, and there will also be boats stored in a smaller shed opposite. The public route on this side of

South Elevation

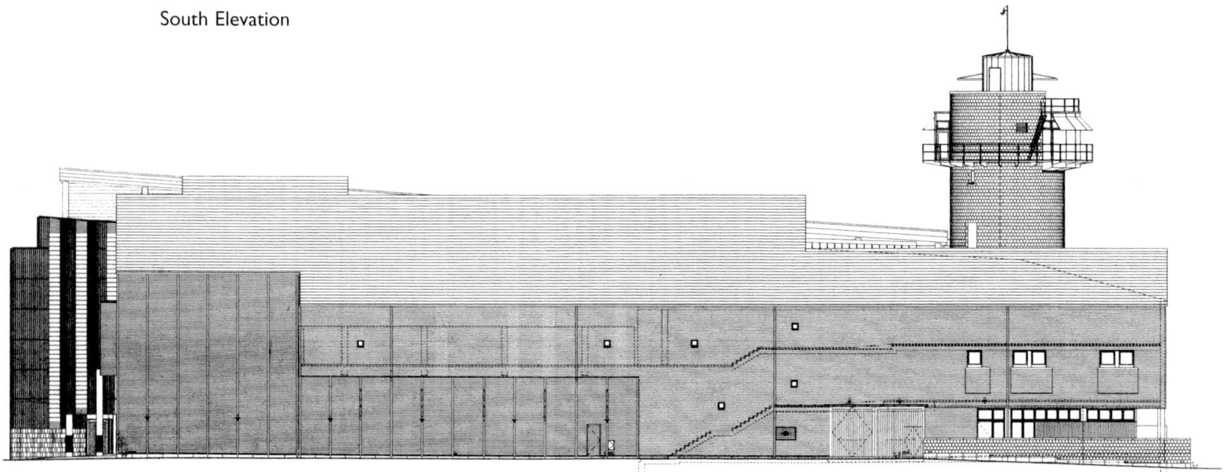

the building leads to the marina, and there is likely to be a ship chandlery in the small square at the end. So the reference to the working history of the site is most appropriate here.

On the other sides of the museum, the palette of materials is the same but the forms and details make it clear that this is not 'just' a boat shed. At the eastern end, where there is open water between the museum

East Elevation

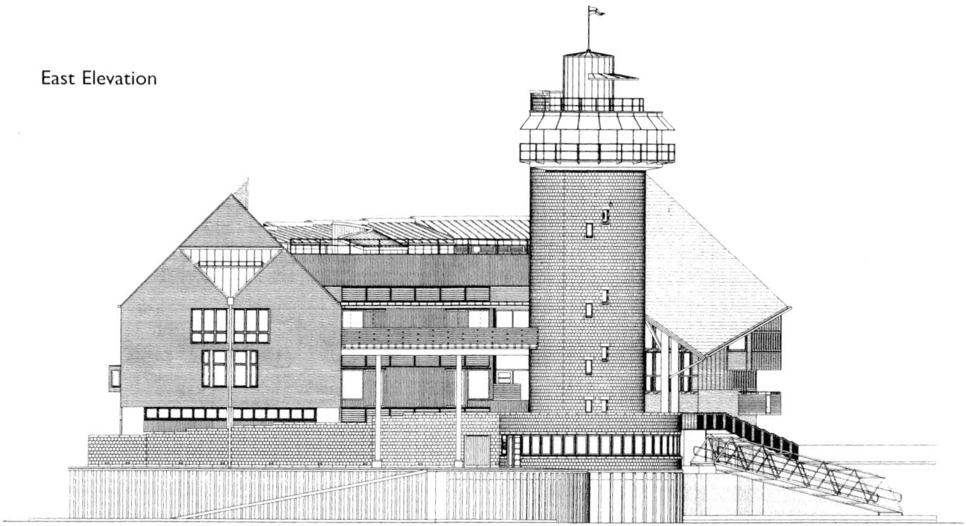

and the docks, the building has a much more open face, with an outdoor balcony for watching sailing demonstrations, and large windows giving views of the water from the museum offices and the large school room. The west end is the entrance and the face of the museum addressing the square and acting as a backdrop for performances. Here the oak has been used in a vertical screen, curved in plan around the entrance, stair, etc. The open screen allows light and air to reach unseen windows behind.

West Elevation

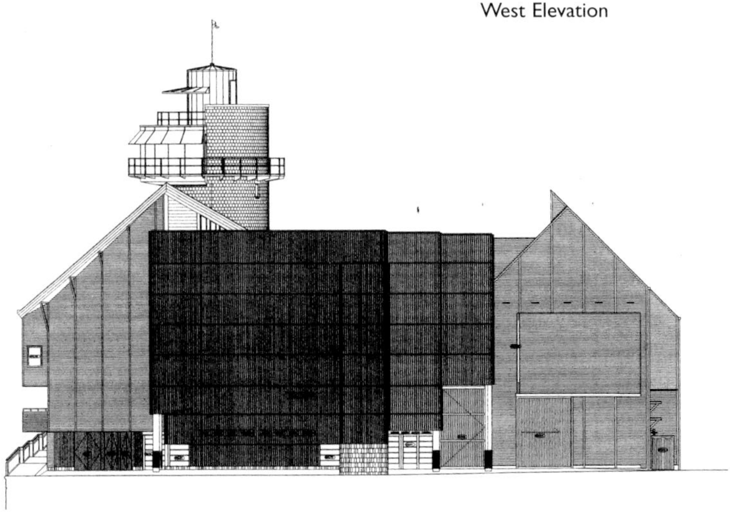

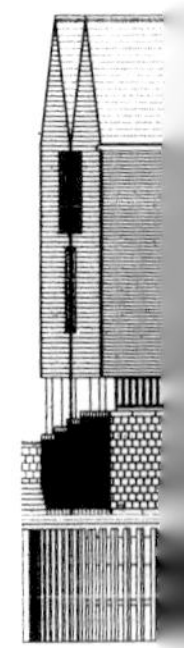

The north facade addresses the harbour and is the most active and vivid of all. It is intended to be read from a distance; to announce itself to the many people who approach the town from the water. On this side the tidal pool creates a dramatic recess in the building, with the outdoor deck and pontoon on one side and the tower on the other. The tower recalls various kinds of waterfront tower, but culminates in a glassy gallery with steel awning.

North Elevation

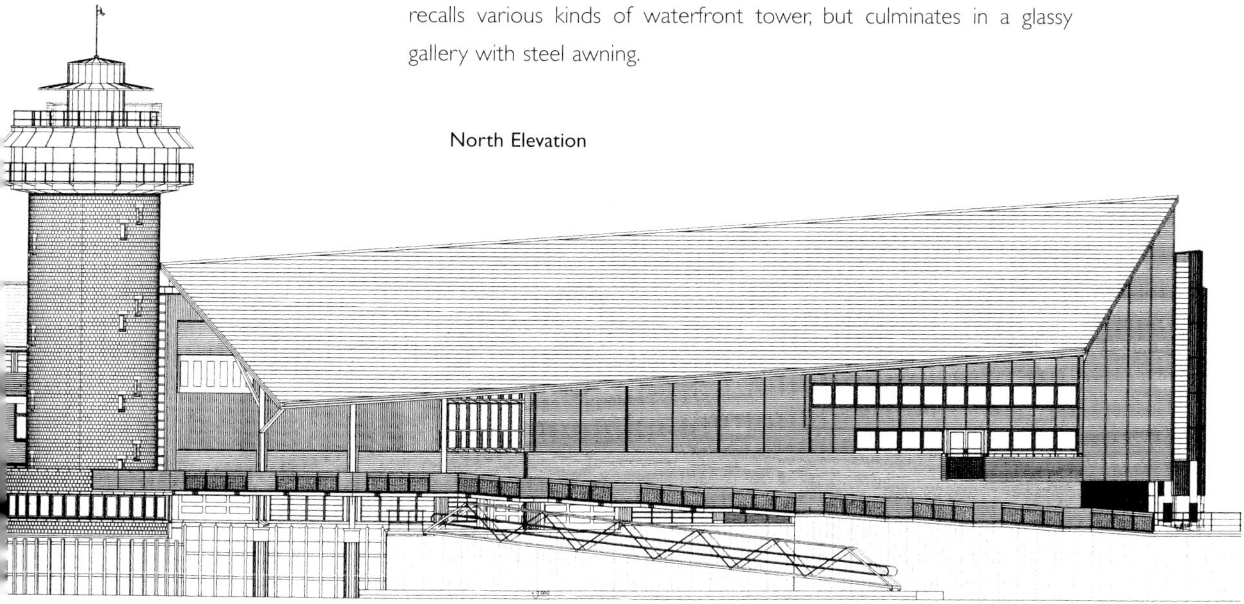

The roof on this side is (perhaps surprisingly) pitched in two directions. This evolved through exploring a number of the issues that had to be resolved on this side of the building. There was a height restriction (which did not, however, apply to the tower) at the eastern end of the site and this determined the maximum roof height at that end of the main building. At the western end, however, it seemed important to make the building high enough to give it some presence on the square, and to allow headroom for a restaurant looking down the length of the Falmouth waterfront. We tried various forms of stepping roof, then decided that simplest was best and that the large scale of an uninterrupted, but tilted, roof slope was the right answer. It seems to us

also to signal the complex balance that this building is trying to achieve between novelty and continuity. On the one hand, it is based on the history of built form on the site, but on the other, by transforming the precedent, it makes it clear that this is not just a boat shed, nor is it a historic building.

Peter Durrant/arcblue

The interests of the museum and the town perhaps come together in their most visible form on the harbour frontage of the museum. A public walkway, accessible to all, tracks around the entire museum. It ramps up over the access from the museum's deck to its pontoon, and from it, people can look into the tidal pool and glimpse the Tidal Gallery and the waterfront model boat pool. The museum is not a sealed private world. It participates in the waterfront and gives something to all visitors, even if they are not paying to go into the museum. The synergy between the life of the Falmouth waterfront, the commercial activities in the square, and the museum experience itself is a conscious part of the design. If we have got it right, they will all gain from the relationship.

This is a new building with an authentic form of its own, which nevertheless takes on the responsibility of being in that place, and creating the next step in a continuing local tradition of building. It refers to Falmouth's past, but without nostalgia, and it gives a form to the museum that is an authentic expression of its operational requirements today.

Andy Campbell